AND SUGAR CRASHES

BY

emily armanios

with Illustrations by
Yvonne Strover

Copyright © 2017 by Emily Armanios

www.emilyarmanios.com

ISBN: 978-0-9945207-2-2

The moral right of the author has been asserted.

All rights reserved.

No part of this publication may be reproduced, distributed, or transmitted in any form or by any means, including photocopying, recording, or other electronic or mechanical methods, without the prior written permission of the publisher, except in the case of brief quotations embodied in critical reviews and certain other noncommercial uses permitted by copyright law.

For permission requests, write to the publisher at the address below.

Kira Armanios Email: Karmanios@gmail.com

Authored by Emily Armanios

Typesetting by Kira Armanios

Cover Artwork by Yvonne Strover

Illustrations by Yvonne Strover

Special Guest Poem by Peter Armanios

Tribute Poems by Peter Adamopoulos

Books may be purchased by contacting the publisher at the above email address.

This is a work of fiction. Names, characters, businesses, places, events and incidents are either the products of the author's imagination or used in a fictitious manner. Any resemblance to actual persons, living or dead, or actual events is purely coincidental.

A CiP catalogue record for this book is available from the

National Library of Australia

For you—
the lovely one holding me in your cooling arms.
Thank you for filling my life with music.

table of contents

- LOVEBIRDS | 9
- FEEBLE DEMANDER | 10
- DASHER | 11
- ROOKIE RISKTAKER | 12
- WADING THROUGH LIFETIMES | 13
- AN HEIR OF ASH | 14
- ON EDGE | 15
- SUNSET EYES | 16
- CADENCE | 17
- THE WAY YOU FILL MY HEART WITH COLOUR | 18
- TOO LATE | 19
- MERCURY | 20
- MY LOLITA | 21
- DANCER | 22
- 23 CLUB | 23
- KISS THE GIRL [GO ON] | 24
- IT HURTS BUT IT AIN'T OUTTA MEANNESS | 26
- UNREASONABLE UNREQUITED LOVE | 27
- CONSEQUENCE | 28
- FAIRY DUST/SWEETENS KISSES | 29
- VENUS | 30
- ALLEYWAY ROSES | 31
- I AM | 32
- PRANCER | 33
- NOTHING ELSE | 34
- IN WORDS OF PEN/POE TRIBUTE | 36
- IMAGINATIVE LONG-DISTANCE LOVER | 38
- DISSONANCE | 39
- EARTH | 40
- REVOLUTION | 41
- BATTERY-POWERED CONNECTION | 42
- FORESIGHT | 43
- VIXEN | 44
- SUMMER GIRLS BRING 'EM | 45
- TIRELESSLY | 46
- PRESSURE | 47
- DREAM | 48
- PUBLIC LISTENER/ADRENALINE FIEND | 49
- MARS | 50
- VOYAGER | 51
- STAYS INSIDE, TROUBLED CHILD | 52
- YOUR MAJESTY | 54

table of contents

COMET	55
HEARTSTRINGS	56
ERASER	58
TAKE A HINT!	59
JUPITER	60
SCATTERBRAINED AND CONFUSED	61
NO STRANGER ARTISTS (COULD THERE BE)	62
CARING LESS WINS	64
THE AGONY OF CHOOSING	65
CUPID	66
HOLY BOOKS	67
WE'RE BOTH INSINCERE BUT I JUST WANT TO BELIEVE YOU	68
HINDSIGHT	69
SATURN	70
LOVE SHY FOR NOW	71
BRING THEM	72
THE BUTTERFLIES DON'T SEEM TO WANT ME	74
WITH YOUR BEARD AND THOSE LIPS	75
STALLING	76
DONNER	77
ZAP!	78
STARBORN	79
URANUS	80
CONSUME	81
DISTRACTED	82
SELF	83
JUST WANT THOSE LETTERS OUT OF YOUR MOUTH	84
DON'T TELL HIM	85
BRAVERY	86
BLITZEN	88
SELF CARE COMES FIRST, BABY	89
NEPTUNE	90
MAGICAL DISCIPLE	91
PARADISE FALLS	92
BAMBI	93
SUNSHINE TERMINAL	94
HYPOTHETICALS	95
HEATHEN	96
THIS YEAR	97
LEARNING OF MARGINAL LOSS IN AN EXCRUCIATING WAY	98
RUDOLPH	99
PLUTO	100

table of contents

DO YOU REALISE YOU'RE DOING IT?	101
LIMERANCE	102
THE IT, THE I AND THE OVER-I	103
BALLERINA BODY	104
RAINBOW HIGHWAY	106
BIRDS AND TREES	107
DYING GIRL LIVES!	108
UNEARTHING HUMAN MYSTERIES	109
UNIVERSE	110
SHOWING PENSIVE SADNESS	111
BEING HOPELESSLY OURSELVES	112
OH, DON'T LOOK AT ME LIKE THAT	114
AM A VICTIM OF IT NONETHELESS	115
DO YOU KNOW ME?	116
THROUGH OCEANIC DISTANCE	117
AUTOPSY, JOHN DOE	118
DARKNESS IN THE WINDOW IN THE MIRROR	119
EARTH 2	120
SOLITUDE	121
CUMMINGS TRIBUTE	122
PROCRASTINATING IN MY DAYDREAMS	124
ICE	125
CAVATIES	126
ALEX	127
GASPING FOR ENOUGH	130
FRIDAY FEVER	131
FINE LINE	132
JUDGEMENT HALL	133
THE LIFETIME TABOO	134
TRIBUTE	135
NOSTALGIA - Greek Version	136
NOSTALGIA	138
MOTHER OF MINE - Greek Version	140
MOTHER OF MINE	141
(THANK YOU)	143

LOVEBIRDS

A perfume so sweet—
every bird within your wake
follows your trail home.

FEEBLE DEMANDER

Familiar, but unsettling...
like I have known you once before—
twice, I'm sure,
or even more.

The next pathetic afternoon we see each other—
would you gently hold my hand?
It's a truly safe demand...

I don't ask for flurries of clothes
or the loss of long-lost innocences...

just the tender holding
of tender hearts in hands.

DASHER

Drag me to the sea—
let us forget about those
dreams we used to dream.

ROOKIE RISKTAKER

Spinning drunkenly around this tavern—
trying to separate my wrongs from my lefts, and
my rights from my... rights?

(Clutching at support beams
like a sailor on a lurching ship)

The music has got me feeling
seven deadly kinds of messed up,
and though I search for moral healing,
I keep on drinking from the cup.

WADING THROUGH LIFETIMES

There is something very
stingy-hot
about the curt words
that fall harshly out of your pleasant lips.

Sensible words, nonetheless,
but carrying with them
an unmistakable bright poison—
as corrosive as acid.

There is an incredible, hefty weight on my shoulders
that squashes my dreams down to a pulp.
Mangles them.
I can tell you're trying to be polite
(oh, let me down easy!)
but I can sense your sharpness and I wonder
why you insist on breaking my heart.

I don't want to be a leech
you feel the need to shake off your leg,
or a growth on you
that spreads

like an infection.

And there's just something so
stingy-hot
about the fact that...

you fill my tummy with butterflies most of the time
but they're slowly being eaten by moths.

AN HEIR OF ASH

attached to the bottle
and drowning in misery...

an absolute cloud of a man—
brooding silently.

heavy and pale and dim
and on the brink of rain.

ON EDGE

Had counterfeit luck
(should'a known I was just buying time)

why do I keep feeling
like
each conversation we have
will be our last?

SUNSET EYES

seeing her
fills me with sunshine

her arms set fire
to my imagination:
dreaming of all the wrong and divine
things
in this world.

and i know nothing
of fatality
or the implications of mortality—
but her eyes
have got me feeling

something very close to that.

CADENCE

My fingers arch uncomfortably,
but I'm smiling something wonderful.
Your words caressing my ears,
as if you're whispering them right into me.

[I can't meet your eyes.]

Your melody *consumes* me,
until
I'm just a string to be plucked,
a note to be played—
a shimmer and a glimmer
in the afternoon shade.

The cadence with which you speak
makes me lose my balance—
a stomach twirling
from your brilliance.

And what we're doing could be misconstrued,
there's a darkness to the air and we both know it:
who will be the first to smash the ice?
Will these platitudes suffice?

I would have kissed you hours ago
but I was afraid

I wouldn't stop.

THE WAY YOU FILL MY HEART WITH COLOUR

the music
is tingling
through me.

i don't pretend to understand the world
but i can *feel* the notes
you're playing

...

like it's another language
i have just become fluent in.

TOO LATE

The rattling of your tin-can heart
against the graveyard of your chest.

Almost like a warning from within:
the soul screaming out—
"beware! beware!
before it's—"

MERCURY

So, rejection is the hole
that rocks you on the highway
and your foot stutters on the brake
but you don't tap— no,
not just yet.

Depression is the wheel
which you steer (but doesn't move)
and your hands grip tight and more,
until your knuckles white and bare.

And the flashing lights disturb you—
but the railway glitters on.
And while the sirens chime through windows
you just turn up your favourite song.

MY LOLITA

My sweet dove,
you are picturesque
in the grotesque burlesque scene—
far more lovely than I could have ever imagined—

like some sort of smoked oak
crackling under the once-warm fire-place;

and I the terrible coldness
that snatches you
from out of your
pool of warmth:
lifting you upwards
and outwards
from under
both armpits.

My tragic *très chic*—
my perfect, sweet girl,
dark circles under your eyes
that no home-brand concealer can erase.

My spectacle beyond seeing—
beyond saving and being—
my bubbly little lollipop-loving creature:
my Lolita.

DANCER

Red velvet adorns her milky thighs
thread and seam on softest skin.

I gazed, in awe, I nearly cried,
and in the morning, purged my sin.

23 CLUB

i'd rather be loved than alive.

KISS THE GIRL [GO ON]

Go on,
you're sitting next to the girl.
Painfully oblivious to the state that she's in—
fixed in place by your moral turmoil.
Do you want to reach out and kiss her? [*Kiss her, kiss her!*]
Do you wish you'd never met her?

Her legs are restless,
and you can't exactly pinpoint why.
The more you think about it,
the more the answer eludes you.
Slipping through your sensibilities,
and disappearing in the mind-mist.

But when she smiles your way,
a wave of *panic* flows through you.
Because she makes you feel exposed!
Like a birthmark bruise or an open wound.
Frankly it makes your heart
stop beating for a moment
but then you remember
to *breathe*.

She *destroys* you when
she looks at you like that.
Like she wants to take you home—
[perhaps she does?]
You push those thoughts out of your head,
because you know it's wishful thinking.

Yet through it all,
you want
to kiss the girl.
[Go on!]

IT HURTS BUT IT AIN'T OUTTA MEANNESS

I was so lucky to have met you
and so lucky to have loved you.
And I'm so thankful that I lost you
in place of never knowing you at all.

UNREASONABLE UNREQUITED LOVE

When we meet, it's like something out of a
poorly-directed movie:
we lock eyes
but we miss each other,
falling back so we may stand with our respective houses—
our homes, our extremely different lives.

So close but so out of reach!
Like Prufrock, singing each to each—
but not to each other...

(and we're not even lovers!)

This is the point in the movie
where the spectators wait eagerly
to see the tension resolved.

This time,
I am the chimera—
of audience and performer.
But there is no uplifting ending
or fizzing fireworks our way—

just school the next day.

CONSEQUENCE

I never thought I would meet you *here*—
in between reckless and admirable:
since *you* are the incarnate
of every spilled secret;
and I the embodiment
of the consequence that comes with it.

FAIRY DUST/SWEETENS KISSES

Okay so now we're at the point—
where you think,
is that really healthy?

And the answer is of course, no,
it goddamn isn't,
and no,
it never was.

But the extreme extent of this lust,
like a snow-fog on a winter's evening
won't seem to dissipate.

I'd like to anticipate
the facial features of your reaction;
the mouth agape,
and eyebrows lifted
and the settling of a pink hue on your face.

Like a newly-waved fairy dust
on the apples of your cheeks.

VENUS

I put shells to my ear so I might hear the sea,
or the mermaids that practice their verses.
And here is the reason I do like with your lips:
I'm seeking the universes.

ALLEYWAY ROSES

Maybe the roses
that spawn into sidewalks
and crowd out the subways
aren't roses at all:

though they are
just as blossoming
and just as graceful,
(they are just as people).

We entwine,
we engage,
react — as roses do:
yet seem to fall flat
on reflection.

Too aware
of our thorns,
and the poisons inside:
too reticent to notice
all the petals that we hide.

I AM

Trying to be open,
and productive, yet still
charming;

but your smile
and your eyes
have been honestly
disarming.

PRANCER

I admire you,
sweet Prancer;

because you are bolder
than the noiseless ones—
you have music
where there should be lungs—

and in life that is golden.

NOTHING ELSE

Oversized coat and scarf,
because it's colder
than you expected.

I, sweltering
in school dress;
jittering with the force
of a thousand wriggling worms—

heart twisting between
stasis
and static.

[don't think I didn't see you
on the far end of the room...]

A voice that hits all the right spots,
and *people*, people everywhere—
barely stopping to admire her
as wholly as I do;
just moving through.

[and there you strum out
her accompaniment—
though I pretended
not to look
at you].

Forward to me,
flustered in the blizzard
of fresh and new but
old and young faces—

all turned towards me
with big, unfilled eyes:
waiting for me to drip the colour
into their skulls
and persuade them to buy
some product or
another, another—

I stutter
mid-way through my speech:
take five point nine *ums* to recover.

Baby,
we are separated by around
two hundred and fifty-six people;
one podium,
one dress,
one oversized coat and scarf,
your slacks, your shirt,

and absolutely nothing else.

IN WORDS OF PEN/POE TRIBUTE

Now let me rant a moment.

I was thinking and over-thinking,
and possibly engaged in some
over-drinking...
and I had an inkling about you
that I couldn't ignore.

My glass was sweaty and I couldn't drink no more.

And as the one that I adore
with all my heart I do implore—
just a moment of your time
and nothing more.

I had so much to say,
before the night turned into day,
but now the stars have flown away—
with an emerging orange-grey...
and hey,
this was no love song—
and though you never did me wrong,
you would be daft to stay so long
inside this cluttered sing-along.

And the moral of the story?
I just hope I wasn't boring—
to the beguiling brink of snoring
in a land of words and pen.

The chance of anger boiling
from the impact, soon recoiling
and thus this was my inkling
I vow I'll never share again.

IMAGINATIVE LONG-DISTANCE LOVER

Monochrome touches,
exploding colour onto us
with every static breath...
we're just a bunch of exposed wires, all set to be disarmed,
locked and loaded or ready to blow;
zipping and zapping in and out of technicolour bliss—
flipping channels like it's nothing, with the white noise hiss...
surrendering these useless vessels we call bodies—

we don't *need* these walking bags of skin and bone
to fully love each other:
my soul wants to possess you, and in turn, be possessed,
and leave my body empty in front of the screen.

DISSONANCE

Is this attraction healthy?
It's barely even legal—
and certainly unethical...
completely indigestible.

Yet still my feelings wander,
of your smile I still grow fonder—
and my poems smell like you now,
which is sweeter than the crowd.

The greed, I feel, is palpable—
like the samba-heartbeat score.
I wish these sins were portable
so I could just stop wanting more.

I know you'll never feel this way!
These thoughts are too bizarre....
so please just strip this heat away
and play me like guitar.

EARTH

This human software is buggy and broken.

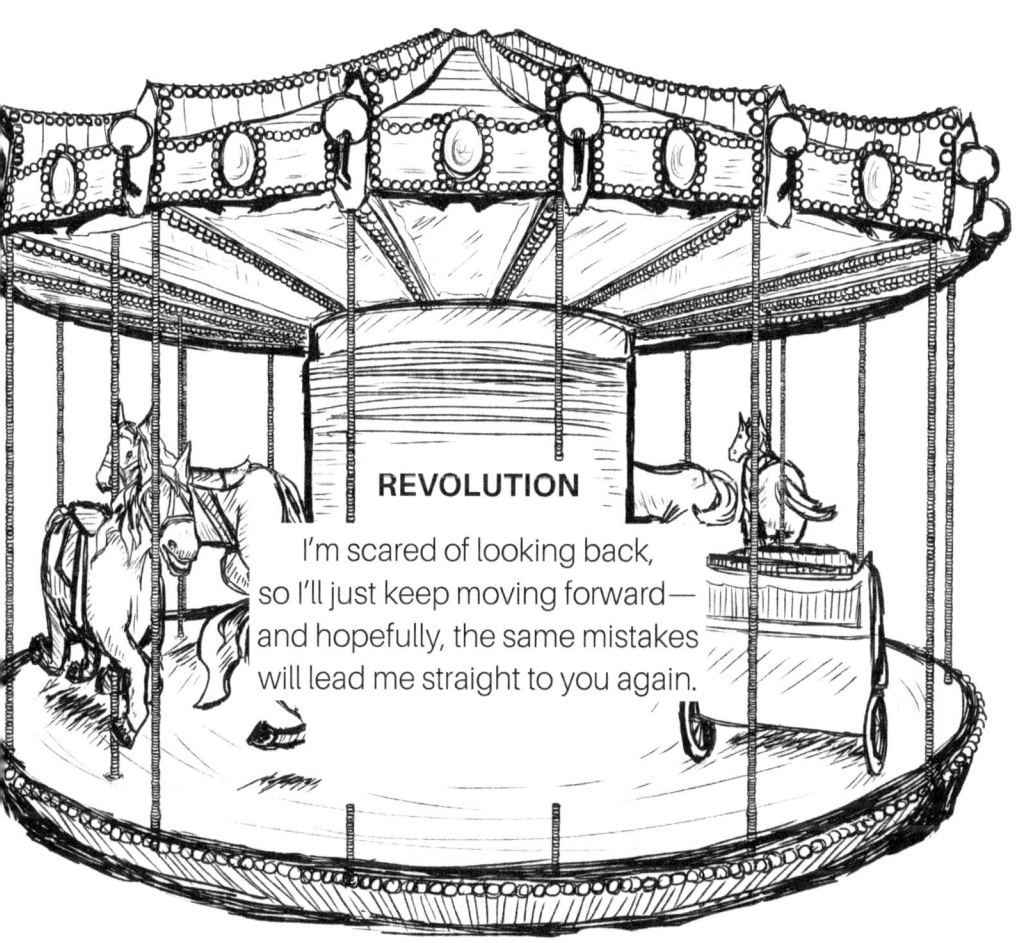

REVOLUTION

I'm scared of looking back,
so I'll just keep moving forward—
and hopefully, the same mistakes
will lead me straight to you again.

BATTERY-POWERED CONNECTION

What happens now,
with both hearts through the telephone pole wires,
unreachable and useless but *electrified?*

Let's just watch
since no one knows—
(at least the sparks
put on a show).

FORESIGHT

If there is one certainty in life,
it is that—
I will always know you love me
so long as you continue to say
hello
in a way that sounds more like
i missed you.

VIXEN

Her body wows me—
I've never seen someone move
like there's a musical hurricane inside them.

Yet there she is,
rolling and dancing,
and so *hotly* alive
(I swear she has a scorching energy).

Everyone watches,
'cause what else are they gonna do?
Mesmerized by the language
that she speaks through fastened lips.

She's *goddamn magnetic*—
inviting attention in her free-spirit.
She's intensely enchanting—
and loving it.

SUMMER GIRLS BRING 'EM

Bring on the Summer!
Give me the right to warm nights—
the shortest shorts humanity has ever known—
the people playing along the shoreline,
your fingers on my hairline.

TIRELESSLY

My hands are writing,
touching,
holding, moving,
creaking, making.

The power is surprising,
and I think
I think
they're breaking.

PRESSURE

Scarves around my neck, and
ties around my wrists—
I like the pressure there, and
I like the way it fits.

DREAM

I had this one dream about you...
and since I can never say these words to your face,
perhaps I can spell them.

It was you—
me—
a bottle of whisky,
temptation sticky in the evening air...
all these thoughts of you I wished to share!

We leaned in,
and I awoke.

PUBLIC LISTENER/ADRENALINE FIEND

I blast off when the crowd calls my name.

Yeah, I get anxious,
and anxious,
and nervous,
but my brain is secretly loving it:

I'm an addict — junkie: something delicious
'bout feelin' absolutely terrified

maybe that's why
I keep crawling back
and confessing stupid shit.

MARS

I have no fear
when I drink beer;
'cause I'm not really here.

VOYAGER

I will lay with
a lone traveller;
and we'll no longer be
alone.

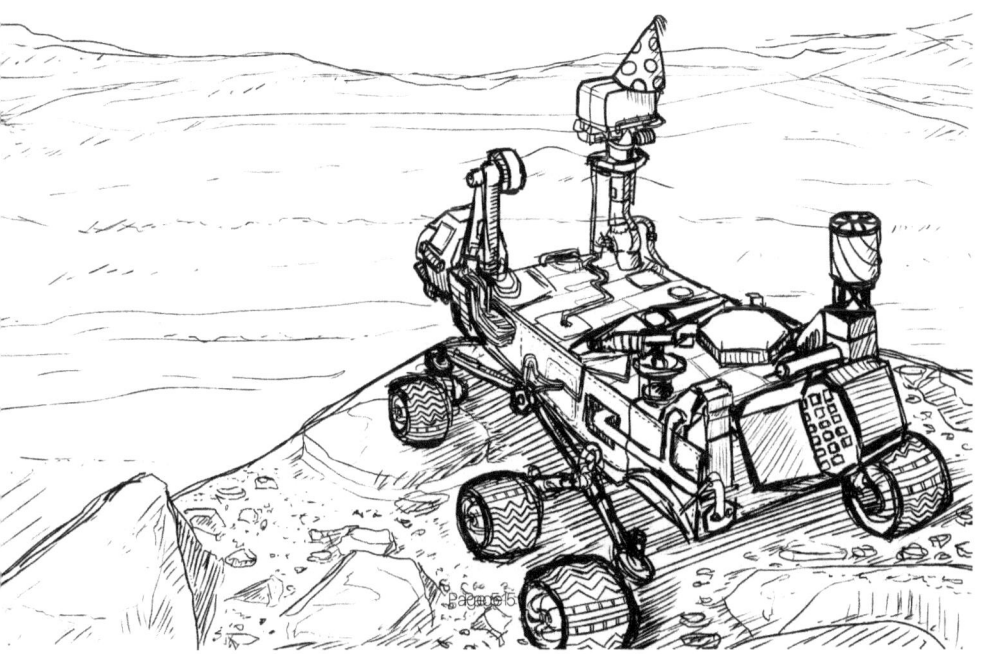

STAYS INSIDE, TROUBLED CHILD

Troubled child is awake;
cobwebs collecting between her fingertips.

All day she wanders through her house,
without really moving—
feather-duster resting on the kitchen-countertop,
covered in the stuff that's it's intended to dispel:
surely there's something ironic in that.

The pads of her fingers trace her abandoned home as if—
(shh!)
as if it might come alive at any time.
Cautious and apologetic for the chaos that her presence
has brought unto it.

The winding, narrow hallways—
lines and lines of wall-hung phones
plastered there and
ringing incessantly...

She is unobtrusive in that fog of noise,
with gentle footfalls that barely
touch the ground.

A living room, empty,
not a single cabinet to rifle through
and explore. Barebones.
She can see the foundation bulging out of the plaster—
an anorexic room to live.
There is nothing to see here.

At least the fire pit's burning;
two parading embers
that seem to flicker left and right.
An uncontrollable burn
enclosed in just
the wrong space.

The bathroom taps don't work,
no matter how much she may turn them,
or how much she cleans out the pipes.

(at least the shower is immaculate)

Is it strange to sit under a shower
that isn't actually running water?
She supposes it doesn't really matter.

With her cobweb fingers and aching ribs,
she wipes the glitter
from her eyes
and with a trembling lip, she sighs.

YOUR MAJESTY

I'm eye level
with the ground
that your shoes are disgracing.

I squint up at you
in hopes of either mercy
or destruction—

on either side
[kissing my cheeks...]

the floor and your muddy boot.

COMET

Troublesome occurrence
in the orange-hot spotlight.

Creativity comes
to a halt.

—stop sign spinning to face me
no matter which intersection point
I approach it from.

Mind wanders to colourful world,
of breathtaking sights that induce tears.

A world which I,
with sunken eyes
can never quite accomplish.

HEARTSTRINGS

"I hope you're a patient person," I say,
as my fingers fumble
and miss their mark again. "Because I'm awful..."

"I'm patient. *Sometimes.*"
You tease me for a moment
and I glance up at you—
startled by your enticing response.
Continue:
"Nah, I'm a patient guy. Don't worry."

"Well, that's a good virtue,"
my voice wavers
and I pluck the strings
to appear busy, "for what you do."
Cryptic...

You hum in approval,
leaning back with your legs
open.

I can't focus on the guitar
and end up making a sour note.
You look up at me
with a dancing amusement
in your eyes.
"Patient, but firm," you explain,
and I'm automatically redirected
to thoughts of you
enacting that firm side upon me.

(these intrusive thoughts race through my head
in the split-second silence)

I echo your statement.
"Patient but firm. In what way?"
Perhaps, secretly,
I'm hoping you'll say—
something indulgent.

"Oh, when the time calls for it."
You wink at me
and I melt
into a puddle on the floor.

A part of me wishes
I could stay here forever,
closed off from the world
while I create my own one
with you.

(I know it's a daydream):
I dream it anyway.

ERASER

Mark my words:
the dawn will kiss you so much sweeter
than that silver
ever could.

TAKE A HINT!

Shit, yeah, I was addicted and obsessed.
Always dressed
like I was goin' to a funeral.
'Cause I thought I might be
at a moment's notice.

You didn't see the arching of my spine,
but I had the heartbeat out on show for you.
Did you realise I was parading for you?

My not-so-subtle subtleties
overshadowing the penalties
fashioned by my wicked hands.

Even though I kept them guarded,
you had to have known
from the way
I *reached* for you.

And yet...

You never said a word—
not one tweet from not one bird:
not known from almond eyes that squint,
I sighed and prayed you'd take a hint.

JUPITER

i start a new contemplation
even though i wasn't yet finished
with the old one.

that's how it goes:
we rush through our thoughts
until none of them make sense anymore.

oh well. i'm just looking for somewhere to rest my tired head—
it's getting too big for my door-frame and bed.

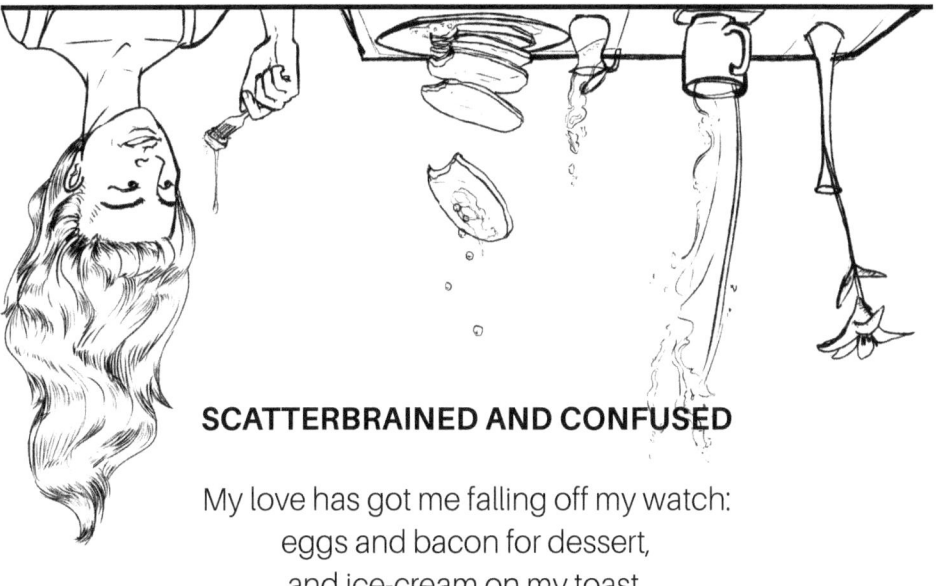

SCATTERBRAINED AND CONFUSED

My love has got me falling off my watch:
eggs and bacon for dessert,
and ice-cream on my toast.

Everything's upside-down
and I don't really mind it—
aside from the fact that all the blood's
rushing to my head,
and it's been rain o'clock for...

seven hours straight.

I'm burning the midnight oil
in the middle of the day,
and that's okay.

NO STRANGER ARTISTS (COULD THERE BE)

Fine, I'll let the green
seep into my life,
and page.

Some stranger
on the train
pointed out
I had ink between my fingers.

For them to have been inspecting me so closely,
I wonder what else had been on their mind—
[was I music to their ears?]

Sure, I was thinking,
while they stood there self-effacing
what it would be like to feel their body heat
but it didn't *mean* anything.
[I had ink between my fingers].

I had the poetic rash start to form on me
from the inside out:
[that was the ink,
beginning to congeal]
liver mortis turning all the good and productive
parts of me
green.

I penned,
in my mind,
the rise and fall of our empire.
Didn't get very far
before us both were beheaded.

Their eyes were bleeding through my clothes—
oh, lovely stranger, had you known,
[I had ink between my fingers]

but I saw your guitar pick
tucked behind your ear.

*

[Two stranger artists meet,
and without moving past a sentence,
have their artistry told unwillingly].

Some things you can't remove from the soul.

CARING LESS WINS

Loneliness inside
this beating heart that's burning
to keep you alight.

THE AGONY OF CHOOSING

Tonight I'm having cherry pie
and apple pie finally,
underneath the disbelief
in fingertips around me—

as I'm grasping for
and asking for
the air to breathe.

Something isn't nothing
and I feel the animosity—
gasping in
and basking in
the scent of foreign bodies.

Maybe if I'm brave enough
to have a little taste-test,
an epiphany will dawn on me
of the flavour that I like best.

Does it need to be exclusive
and definitely definite?
If I could choose, baby, I would,
but my ecstasy is infinite.

CUPID

break the windows and climb right in.

i'm inviting you now
(since hinting
wasn't enough).

HOLY BOOKS

You look at me like
I'm the oasis in your desert,
a mirage in front of your eyes.

I gain confidence
from the way
your glances seem
like an indulgence.

Now I am willing to relinquish
any semblance of power—
bowing to my feet
and folding myself in half.

Ironic, the way you look at me, because...

The angels have tried
to recapture your features
in their holy books
for some time now.

But always stopping and stalling
at the first strand of hair.

**WE'RE BOTH INSINCERE BUT
I JUST WANT TO BELIEVE
YOU**

Our polka dots bright
like stars in the sky
and dotting each lie.

HINDSIGHT

Though I do sometimes wonder
if you ever think about me
since the last time
we really spoke.

It was honestly quite telling
and I should have seen it coming
when I said, "well, see you later",
but you only said goodbye.

SATURN

robotic limbs
and a cubic head.

yes, this is how
we're doing business (love)
from now on.

butterfly fluttering
around his robotic palm.
shh.

his hand's not yet finished—
and it's often prone to twitches.

LOVE SHY FOR NOW

one by one
i've been leaving
my pens inside your office

hopefully, some day
i'll have no more of my pens left
(and will have to ask to borrow one from you).

when that time comes,
i hope that i am brave enough
to ask you on a date.

BRING THEM

Bring them this hot, melting Summer,
with dry humid rains
that coat the lashes in tiny drops.

Bring them the lush green land
on their bright red fingertips—
bursting
with some type of new creation:
like flowers blooming
in the garden of imagination.

Bring them the ultimate delight
of being:
give them that warm, concentrated
feeling
of being so absolutely full.
Bring them the sunshine in the form of
thousand-watt smiles,
bring them the chance to fall in love
at the lowering of a gaze
and voice.

Bring them a twisting rash that burns their middle,
from the inside-out;
that turns them—
upside-down;
bring them the time-melting,
brain-exploding,
leg-buckling touch
that staves off the hungry beast—
give them some awestruckedness.

Bring them that cool delicious feeling
of sliding over cucumber-fresh skin
with their *tongue*,
bring them that shuddery sensation,
like the sprouting of Angel wings
on spines.

Give them the prickle of tears behind their eyes,
give them the wilting flowers in the vase,
leaves burdened by toxins—
gently falling to the ground.

Give them those words
that cannot be taken back,
give them the tears
that cannot be unshed;
give them the rips and holes
in the interior furniture of the mind—
which cannot be
remade.

Give them all of this, and
they will understand love.

THE BUTTERFLIES DON'T SEEM TO WANT ME

Have I overstayed my visit?
Was there enough left to explore?
Their flutters so exquisite—
had I not been bold before?

I thought my heart was big enough
to shelter every wisp—
the safety coming more undone
with each wing that I kissed.

WITH YOUR BEARD AND THOSE LIPS

You're reminding me
of chocolate on cherry,
and to think of taste
in sweets and berries
is a very lovely thing indeed.

STALLING

you drive me home
and i pray for red lights.

DONNER

Warm evening night, with lights and
the scent of you—
all over me.

Who knew we were surrounded by other people?
I shiver at your smile,
laughing breathlessly—
nervously,
wondering if you caught the longing in my voice.

The party air is so loud,
I can barely see you.
And then;
my face etched in horror or desperation
or a mixture of the two—
(I think she knew).

Her hands, her lips, breaking the concentration
we have on each other—
we fall apart like asbestos-filled walls,
the dust escaping and polluting the room—
who knew we were surrounded by other people?

She is *nothing* that I was or am or ever will be—
and the party ended years ago
in the hours since we all left:
sinking like we never have to die,
but our dreams do not condone our lies.

ZAP!

Helpless and weary,
I found myself crying—
for all that I'd never felt.

The light came in streaming
like sunshine through ribcage,
and deep in submission, I knelt.

The sound was electric—
strung up all around me:
so I danced with the voice I was dealt.

STARBORN

And the stars have been calling out to you for years:
"we are yours, we are yours, we are yours"—
and *"when will you start believing us?"*

URANUS

Gentle and agile drops.
A pounding skull tries to reset the cloudy brain inside it.
Hungry (yearning?) sighs the culprit.

The diamond deluge just keeps on comin'.
But...

The rain does not blur your features, gorgeous.
Not even floods could thin your sweetness.

CONSUME

Stomach is barren
fill it to burst—

so you can feel
pain and
better soon.

Ease your worries,
but murder yourself—

not with a gun,
but with a spoon.

DISTRACTED

Desperately explore...
immoral thoughts — discipline:
snaps the guitar string.

SELF

Objectivity died
when man created mirror.
Ironically enough, the mirror
could finally make man
as fully and completely
full and complete
as man
knew himself to be.

Outside validation
is now treated like a drug—
sold at every corner
and opportunity—
and blatantly
on social media.

How funny to believe
our self-worth can be determined
by others
who are most certainly not
the self in question—

how funny to think
we are limited by
what's expected of us.

JUST WANT THOSE LETTERS OUT OF YOUR MOUTH

Nothing hurts like this does.
So why can't I do something about it?

I feel *trapped*,
captured,
just a helpless drowning bird
in the ocean of your gravity.

Can't help but want to stay in motion with ya,
while you just want to be stagnant.

And I don't wanna appear too eager—
like my atoms are vibrating much faster than yours are:
causing the hotness of my cheeks
and the chill of your demeanour.

DON'T TELL HIM

This affair has gotten out of hand,
out of mouth, of skin, of flesh—
it's seeping in to the soul,
and (I don't think) I can
resist.

BRAVERY

Today, in the morning,
I accidentally spoke a fact
[of poetry]: "I think the more embarrassing it is,
the more important it is
to write about."

It wasn't until today, in the evening,
I understood how right it was.

Springing forth from a justification,
came a riveting downright revelation.

In a thousand years' time,
how will the human condition
be accurately assessed,
and pitied, and pondered,
and obsessed over,
if there is nobody writing the embarrassing stuff?

Addressing and caressing it
and sharing it with the unreceptive crowd
who turn their heads in flushed horror?

I don't claim that I'm the gatekeeper
to the pure white bars of truth:
I just think that it's important
to be brave and without ruth.

So write about what scares you!
Scribble down what makes you blush.
Detail all your biggest fears—
and feel the written rush.

Write about the honest things,
like guilty pleasures
and crushes on teachers—

and look back in fifty years
and see yourself in honest pictures.

BLITZEN

The day feels cooler
than it actually is—

must be those eyes
that are piercing my skin.

SELF CARE COMES FIRST, BABY

You are the conductor of a mind-symphony
in the middle of a brain-garden:

and you are so important,
more than you could ever know—

dearest,
just be sure to water those flowers

(like the fruits of ideas)

NEPTUNE

I know the seas don't own me
in this tiny wooden boat—
but it's both comforting and scary
that I'm somehow still afloat.

MAGICAL DISCIPLE

Okay, fine,
confession time;
I'd like to wrap myself up
in your coat.

And stay there,
and stay,
and lay there,
all still.

I've seen that trench,
have watched you go
(with saddened eyes)
I saw it follow:

and like your coat,
I want to flow;
down whatever path
that you may sew.

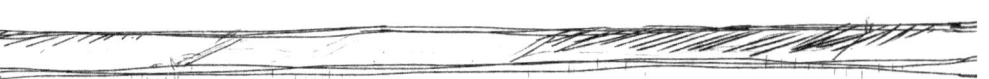

PARADISE FALLS

I am wishing for
tropical beaches,
palm trees,
cold drinks
and warm hands.

BAMBI

have any words
in any tongue
been so completely
sweetly sung

than words of those
in deep despair—
in trembling fear
and faux-repair?

destroyer blind
by wrathful rage
and tiny lamb
in smaller cage—

help is nowhere *near*
what you need,
darlin'.

SUNSHINE TERMINAL

The sun makes haste in its warming glow, to
shield and protect all the contents within—
like an open box of confetti-children,
while humanity forfeits its knuckles.

The noiseless colour that flits through the sky
in order and wave and catastrophe—
has not broken its promise, thought much of
it will — return back to sea; return back
to see.

HYPOTHETICALS

If I asked to be hurt—
would you bite me?

If I asked to be healed—
would you kiss me?

If I asked to be killed...
would you love me?

HEATHEN

Daily delivery of privileged issues...
talks of too much love
and how there's always enough food to eat.

The lyrics by now are overused and fuzzy—
need some bourbon
to bring me back
to reality.

*"Just forget about your troubles
and come join me here in bed!"*

Oh, babe...

if only truth were in those words
that could be so Heaven-sent.

THIS YEAR

Trades birthday candles
for wishes and kisses and
more birthday candles.

LEARNING OF MARGINAL LOSS IN AN EXCRUCIATING WAY

I live for those tender moments
where you let down your guard
and invite me in.

Oh, when you touch your single index finger
gently on my knee
(accidentally!)

How fast and wild my thoughts ran
with the pulsating desire
for you to clasp your entire hand
around my trembling joint—

almost delirious with the impulse
to keen and barter with you
for some more depth of connection.

My breathing was shallow and intense,
though I'm not sure you noticed it then,
as your finger departed from my bare and rosy skin—

I inwardly cried a river of tears
before the loss could settle in.

RUDOLPH

her red lip
she bites
(when she lies— 'cause
she thinks i can't tell).

when she cries,
all i see
are those crocodile eyes.

PLUTO

stepping stones—
these pretty rocks

tell
me
where
to
go.

i have no idea who laid you down,
but lead the way, stranger.

DO YOU REALISE YOU'RE DOING IT?

Please,
brush my leg with yours again.

Oh, your touch isn't liberal
but it's enough to entice me
entrap, ensnare

and ultimately
deceive me.

LIMERANCE

Sisyphus ceaselessly rolling the rock
up to the top of the hill—

only to watch as it rolls back down
despite his blazing will.

Now I've heard of retribution
and the spirit it does kill,

it might be vain to spot the difference,
but to me it sounds like limerance.

THE IT, THE I AND THE OVER-I

The best part about dating a writer:

not the tea around the clock,
or the musings and the laughter—
but the fact that you're immortalised
in every poem after.

BALLERINA BODY

Tonight we met in a whirlwind of colours.
Me in black and you in grey and white...
...and red and blue and pink and red and pink.
And you were straight up and down, but leaned towards my way,
and my curves hugged my dress but my body was stiff.

You expected a kiss fleetingly,
I, surprised,
took your cheek a minute as my prize—
you were a hot, angry fire,
burning brighter than the candles around the table.
And for the minute I was able...
I thought about you underneath your clothes,
and I still
am thinking about it.

Ripe and young and tender,
from sixteen years of tiptoeing to sad French music.
I'm not ashamed,
but it makes it harder to sleep.
If you were here, I'd ask you more:

about your mother, your father; I'd ask you
when the last time you cried was.
I'd watch your mouth move and wonder
what it'd be like to kiss such supple lips.
I'd get lost in your voice and imagine
your muscled ballerina body against my soft, untrained one
and ask you
what it felt like to contain a galaxy
in those legs that were made to dance.

Ask you if you ever looked at other people's legs
and wonder how they wandered.
I'd ask if I could say your name and have you say mine back.
Oh, I'd have asked you so many things.
I wanted to know about the scar on your shoulder,
and whether you knew if it was endearing
or not.

I'd answer your questions, too,
if you ever had any.
Speak truthfully and with earnest,
speak earnestly and with truth—
even if the lump in my throat only got bigger.

All this happened before my eyes,
our lives
unfolded
like I was watching a highlight reel.
But how silly to believe
that there could be anything between us.

Silently I watched
as you tip-toed upstairs,
your grace like a fox,
and folded back in
to your musical box.

RAINBOW HIGHWAY

Double-bent
and backwards, flying
through the open road—

the journey is long,
but I've
a whole playlist
to keep me company.

BIRDS AND TREES

Waiting here for you...
wondering if birds and trees
listen like us too.

DYING GIRL LIVES!

We're all dying.

Right now, at this very moment.

We are steadily heading towards
our inevitable demise, so...

uh, amongst the chaos—
the niceties and unspoken feelings,
the cosmos is telling us all
to be brave and stupid and lovestruck

and I've never been one to defy the cosmos...

I'm trying to say
that I don't have enough Earth-minutes left
to describe all the reasons
your smile's making me feel
stupid and brave and lovestruck.

I have to chase these feelings
and these
confessions of desire, because...

I guess I just want to spend
my dying time with you.

UNEARTHING HUMAN MYSTERIES

People don't move in ways they understand,
which is scary.

[But it's not all that complicated.]

We're all just gorgeous, restless things,
making wishes on stars,
flowers,
and candles—
hoping (   ) will pass us by.

UNIVERSE

If destiny is the divining force,
then so be it: stars,
re-arrange yourselves
into constellations I cannot decipher:
I will still find my way
by the eyes.

If the patterns in the clouds the future tell,
then so be it: rain
make my head heavy with your tears
and I shall still look up
to meet you.

You see,
I hold tomorrow in my hands—
and no natural energy
can dampen me.

SHOWING PENSIVE SADNESS

A bag filled up with desert sand
and handfuls of the ocean—
if you may find a cup of world,
please pour in my direction.

BEING HOPELESSLY OURSELVES

Let's go backpacking through mountains
(and forget our cameras)!
So we can rely on the processors
in our heads.

Let's go and drive around the country
(because we hate our jobs).

Let's take a trip
in a hot-air balloon
and point out the tiny cars
(like ladybugs)!
scuttling along their planned roads—
whilst we command the skies.

Let's start a murder-mystery novel
and leave the mystery a mystery—
so the readers get to the end
and want to take a lighter to the pages...
but recommend it to their friends
with muted rage.

Let's compose a song and never release it
but pretend that we were mega-stars.
And joke about our success
as we eat from take-out containers
on the floor of an empty house

Let's dance in the streets
to professional busker's blues
and invite strangers to waltz with us
(waving kindly
when they refuse).

Let's dye our hair and chop it off,
get tattoos and instantly regret them,
embrace the temporary permanence
of the ink on our decaying flesh
and move on with our lives.

Lets wake up in the AM
and go running through the streets
bike-riding and picnic-having
while we're only lit up by the stars
and the fire in our eyes.

Let's live.
And when we're dead,
let's rest.

Knowing
there's not a thing more
we could have been
than

hopelessly ourselves.

OH, DON'T LOOK AT ME LIKE THAT

Melodies come true
in that dazzling gaze of yours—
I forget my name.

AM A VICTIM OF IT NONETHELESS

The head outhinks the heart.

Drastically, frantically, putting up walls
that no explorer
can ever tear down.

Exactly like a precautionary measure—

trying to get as close as possible to eternal safety
(but that isn't what moves me).

DO YOU KNOW ME?

Baby blue-eyed boy—
I know you.
(as intimately as)
you know you.

I know your tricks,
I know your whys,
I know the colour
of your sighs—

I know what turns you
upside-down
(I understand)
that soulful frown.

I know you,
blue-eyed boy,
(I just wish I knew you
better).

THROUGH OCEANIC DISTANCE

Someone stop your energy
from hitting me:

(I feel you
no matter how many miles
of muck and sand are between us—)

Collecting feelings
like they're stardust.

AUTOPSY, JOHN DOE

Are you tipsy or topsy?
We may need an autopsy.

DARKNESS IN THE WINDOW IN THE MIRROR

thunder
beating
through the window

lightning
in the
mirror striking

possessed
no more
demons inside.

'cause they were standing
right
in front of me.

EARTH 2

I'm lying on my postcards.

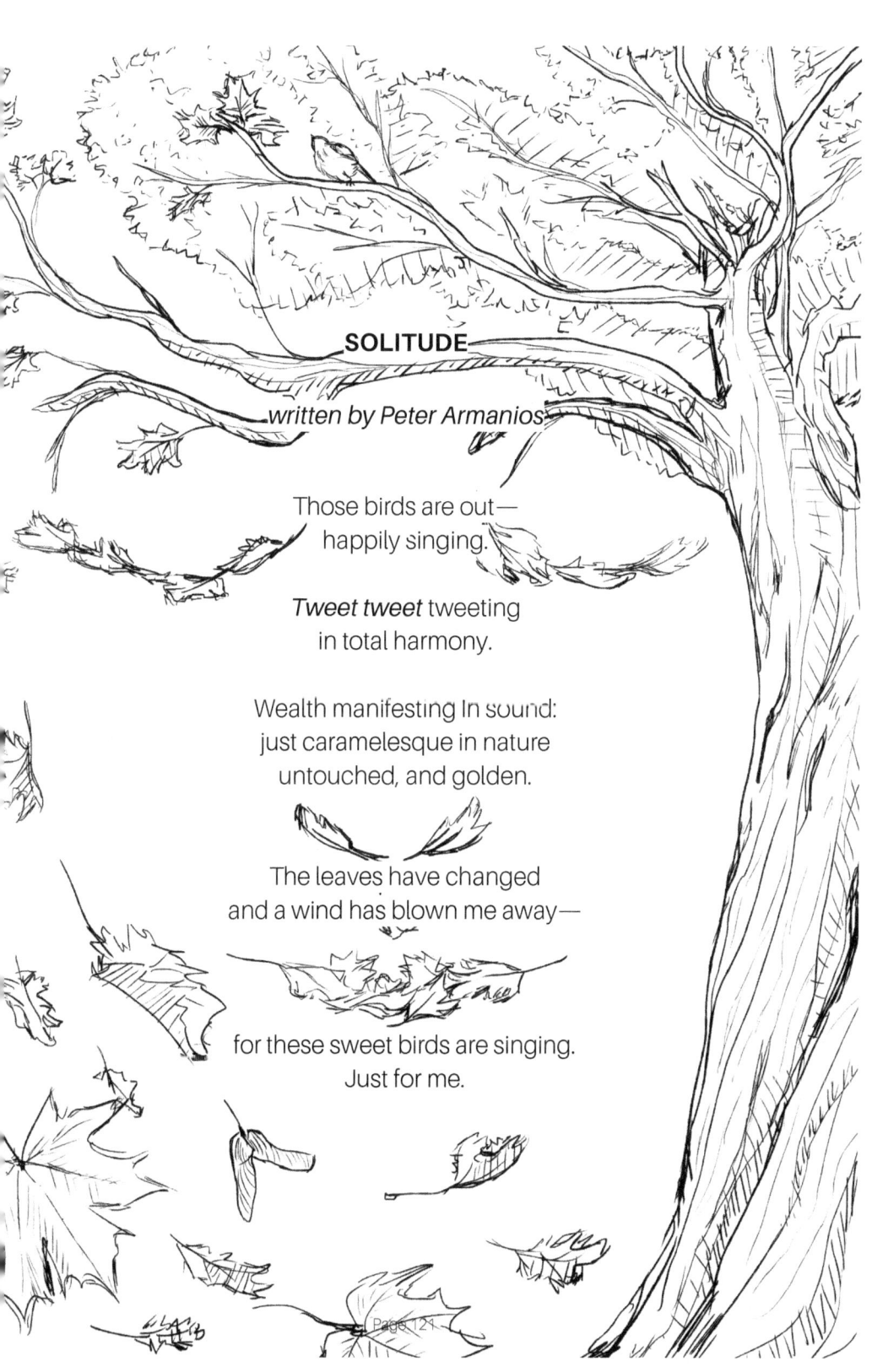

SOLITUDE

written by Peter Armanios

Those birds are out—
happily singing.

Tweet tweet tweeting
in total harmony.

Wealth manifesting In sound:
just caramelesque in nature
untouched, and golden.

The leaves have changed
and a wind has blown me away—

for these sweet birds are singing.
Just for me.

CUMMINGS TRIBUTE

walking home one night,
watching strangers pass through me
all hands all held.

was distracted, so i did
not see the
puddle
i was about to step in.

(i stepped in it)

pulling tendrils of my hair upward
the water jetted into the sky
(no, that's not right)
it was i
falling downwards.

closed my eyes
out of fear—
but after a moment,
peeped one open.

the Underwater Kingdom
was before me:
so joyous, from my ducts
came tears to mingle with the air.

population: eighty billion
said the neon sign
up to my right.
hello, hi, said everyone
that passed my body's light.

because all was water,
nothing was,
relatively.

i did not need to hold my breath
any more.
my greedy lungs astounded.

but all in a moment,
i was coming back down—
twirling back in
to my pretty how town.

PROCRASTINATING IN MY DAYDREAMS

There is so much left to see and do,
yet still I lie and sigh for you.

ICE

Meeting you
was like icing a bruise:
singeing, but intensely satisfying.

Loving you
was like icing a cake:
sugary sweet and decadent.

Leaving you
was like icing a person:
living, and then
assuming room temperature.

CAVATIES

Candy is great for sweeter-feeling dreams,
sugar hearts falling apart at the seams.
But in the day,
they fade away—
to bitterness, it seems.

ALEX

In these little works of mine,
I will always (without fail)
have the utmost of trouble
trying to describe you
with mortal words.

Some synonyms come immediately to mind
when writing about you:
handsome, generous, kind—
but these words are so generic and bland—
overused and void of any real meaning...
it's almost insulting to have your name
and their phonetic clusters in the
same sinking sentence.

I know that it would feel
one billion times better
to *make up* some words about you.
But I'm not sure where I would begin.

How do I start to describe somebody
who could light up the recesses of space
if he ever felt so inclined?
I can't correctly label you.
Can't detail your peachflame skin,
or the silky smoothness of your bare arms, chest, legs... hm.

How do I describe your maltibon eyes—
glistening and flickering from one exciting scene to the next,
roaming all over the brilliance of the world in front of you—
scurrying over my frame temptuously
(eagerly but with caution);
afraid to break something telepathically;
bound to devour everything inside
those black-hole pupils? How?

Is there a shortcut into your mind
that could allow me to possess every inch of your thoughts?
Let me peek inside that troubled place, dear—
I want to see what keeps you up at night.
I would pay with all my life
to feel the grey matter of your brains.

My love for you— sweet creature of disaster,
breaker of hearts,
stealer of shows,
taker of breaths—
runs deeply,
in a vein far too ground-emburied to ever be exposed
with stone or diamond.

But rambling gets me nowhere!

Let me give you a final thought;
a goodbye.
It will only be as temporary
as the sun or moon
to one side of the Earth.

My love for you is eternal—
unfathomably wide and long and dense
as the universe itself.

When all the buildings on this planet
shudder and collapse,
there shall be my love still;
and when there is no heart left beating,
there shall be my love still.

If there ever comes a time
where you shall find yourself
fit to leave—
pack those metaphorical and metaphysical bags
to take on some new type of Everest,
through all the ruin and the rags:
there shall be my love still.

GASPING FOR ENOUGH

"Wounds don't heal until you stop pressing them," you say.
"So stop touching," I breathe.

FRIDAY FEVER

Oh, my god,
I saw you this afternoon.
We were all shy and cold in the little Winter room!

But your eyes were ocean, ocean alive;
wide
and bursting
with your own personal fire—

you were like the beach I forever wanted to sunbathe on:
with crystal-clear waters and silky white sand

and the syllables that were softly sloping from your open lips,
ah, like wine I drank them in; your lexis I indulged in tiny sips.

And now I am in a relentless loop
of remembering you, remembering you.

And wanting to go back to that moment
where our eyes had locked
and your hands had shook
with some kind of excess adrenaline.

The bell rang and I was not yet ready to leave
my hands were still itching to get back to you—
as I stood, my nails embedded in the wooden desk
with the force remaining crescent moons.

FINE LINE

Step one: you shift the focus out
obscuring edge and line.
Step two: you scream and cry and shout
as truth and lies entwine.

JUDGEMENT HALL

eh, they look at me and ask:
is it permanent?
or can we find our way
out of this mess?

...

seriously, you're asking me?
yesterday i learned to walk
and i'm still trying to balance my gait.

i dunno what they told you, pal;
i'm just gonna keep on smiling
and slide by unassuming.

THE LIFETIME TABOO

I don't know if you believe in Heaven,
above those clouds in sky-wedge blue—
but I know you'll find your halo
from the Heaven within you.

TRIBUTE

Written by Peter Adamopoulos

&

Translated by Tabitha Kotsabouikis

Miss You, Papou.

ΝΟΣΤΑΛΓΙΑ

Εψές ο ήλιος έδυσε
Στην άγια μου πατρίδα
Κι έναν τού΄δωκαν φίλημα
Σε θλιβερή αχτίδα
Να μου το φέρει εμένα

Θέλω να δω την μάνα μου
Τ΄αδέλφια μου να φιλήσω
Στον τάφο του πατέρα μου
Θέλω να προσκυνήσω
Βαρέθηκα τα ξένα

Μικρό, μικρό μ΄ορφάνεψε
Η αλύπητη μου μοίρα
Μικρό, μικρό της ξενιτιάς
Το μονοπάτι πήρα
Με χείλη πικραμένα

Μα τώρα πια το χόρτασα
Της ξενιτιάς τα κάλη
Αν είναι και παράδεισος
Θα την αφήσω πάλι
Βαρέθηκα τα ξένα

Μικρό χελιδονάκι μου
Για μια στιγμούλα στάσου
Για μια στιγμή λυπήσουμε
Και δώς μου τα φτερά σου
Τα λεπτοκαμωμένα

Θέλω το δίστιχο και γω
Στο σπίτι μου να πάω
Θέλω στης μάνας το πλευρό
Λίγο ψωμί να φαγω
Βαρέθηκα τα ξένα

Ανδρειωμένα μου βουνά
Για λίγο χαμηλώστε
Για λίγο, λίγο κλείνετε
Λίγο βοήθεια δώστε
Σε πόδια κουρασμένα

Πεθύμησα να στολιστώ
Με γιορτινό στυλίδι
Να πάω στην πατρίδα μου
Στ'αγαπητό ταξίδι
Βαρέθηκα τα ξένα

Στο εξωκλήσι τ Άγιου Λιά
Να πάω να προσκυνήσω
Να δω τους φίλους τους παλιούς
Μαζί τους να γλεντήσω
Με γνήσιο κρασί απ'το χωριό
Κόκκινο και ρετσίνα
Και με τραγούδια όμορφα
Βαρέθηκα τα ξένα

NOSTALGIA

Yesterday the sun set
on my holy homeland
a kiss was given
through a saddened rays
to reach me

I want to see my mother
to kiss my sisters and my brother
And pay worship
to the grave of my dear father
I'm sick of all that's foreign

I was orphaned very young
a cruel fate
leaving me solitary on the path
to these foreign lands
with lips embittered

I have satisfied my hunger
with all the riches of this foreign country
even if it's truly paradise
I would leave it in a heartbeat
I'm sick of all that's foreign

My little baby swallow
stop for just one moment
for just one moment show me pity
and lend me your petite wings

I want this poem and me
to fly back to my home
I just want to be by my mother's side
a bit of bread to eat where I belong
I'm sick of all that's foreign

Lower yourself just a little
my mountains, so very brave
little by little you close yourselves off from me
send just a little aid
to these exhausted legs

I miss dressing myself up
for my village's feast
I want to take
the beloved journey home
I'm sick of all that's foreign.

At Saint Elia's chapel
I want to go and kneel
and see my friends of old
and laugh with all who find us
with genuine wine from the village
so splendid, red and resin
and to sing songs too beautiful to forget
I'm sick of all that's foreign

ΜΑΝΑ ΜΟΥ

Ο΄μάνα μου σ΄ευχάριστω
Μπροστά σου γονατίζω
Σεμνά τα πόδια σου φιλώ
Και άθελα δακρύζω

Τόσα πολλά που σου χρωστώ
Τόσα που μου΄χεις κάνει
Οσο και αν πω ευχάριστώ
Να πληρωθείς δε φτάνει

Εκεί μαζί με τον Χριστό
Δίπλα στην Παναγία
Σεμνά το κάδρο σου κρατώ
Μανούλα μου αγία

Και όρκο σου κάνω όσο ζω
Ποτέ μη σε ξεχάσω
Και τη γλυκιά σου τη μορφή
Πάντα στην σκέψη μου θα έχω

Μάνα μανούλα μου γλυκιά
Μάνα ευλογημένη
Μάνα μορφή αγγελικιά
Και πολύ αγαπημένη

Καλό σου ταξίδι
Αιωνία σου η μνήμη

MOTHER OF MINE

O mother of mine, I thank you
Before you I fall to my knees
Respectfully, I kiss your feet
Weeping unexpectedly

I owe you so much
You have done so much for me
No matter how much I say thank you
The debt could never be repaid

There united with Christ
With the Virgin Mary, in line
Respectfully I hold your picture
Saintly mother of mine

And an oath I'll take while I'm alive
to never forget you
And your sweet appearance
I'll have it always in my mind

Mother of mine, sweet mother
Blessed mother
Angelic, saintly mother
And much beloved mother

I wish you the best on your journey
May your memory be in eternal glory

thank you

You know a project has been a real beast when you have a whole page of people to thank and acknowledge.

To these people, thank you dearly for turning this dream into a reality. I'd like to thank—

Mum,
Thank you for your unflinching support even when I was at my peak primadonna; it's hard for me to put into words the sheer appreciation I have for you— all I have are these intangible, elusive feelings of deep gratitude— splotches of emotion that cannot transcend the heart to form words on a page— all I have are open arms for you, Mum.
For ever,

Dad, for teaching me that everything is always within my reach;
Helen, for breathing joy into my writing;
Peter, for swelling my heart with pride;
Grandpa, for lending some of your sensitivity;
Alex, for (always) fuelling this fire;
Tabitha, for your precious contribution;

Yvonne, thank you for your profound illustrations that physicalize all the emotions I've been trying to articulate. You have made this process intensely enjoyable and exciting, and it is a tremendously high honour to be able to call you a partner in crime. I hope you are proud of the art you have made because it is utterly immortal. I love you.

And lastly, Thank You, for supporting this book's creation.
Thanks for stopping by - I hope to see you again soon.

AND SUGAR CRASHES

By *emily armanios*

Deeply moving and now with the added intricacies of professional illustrations, **And Sugar Crashes** is the syrupy sequel to *Of Lips and Lashes.*

Featuring poems largely inspired by infatuation, music and genuine introspection, this spellbinding collection pushes poetic boundaries — dabbling into experimental, narrative and tribute poems to demonstrate temporal artistic growth and a willingness to share pure vulnerability in unabashed words and striking images.

Open, authentic and inviting, this anthology of over 120 charming poems intends to linger in the thoughts of every reader, even well after they have been read, re-read and bookmarked.

Published by Kira Armanios

www.ingramcontent.com/pod-product-compliance
Lightning Source LLC
Chambersburg PA
CBHW070808230426
43665CB00017B/2537